Mysterious Sea Monsters
of California's Central Coast

Randall A. Reinstedt

Illustrated by
Ed Greco

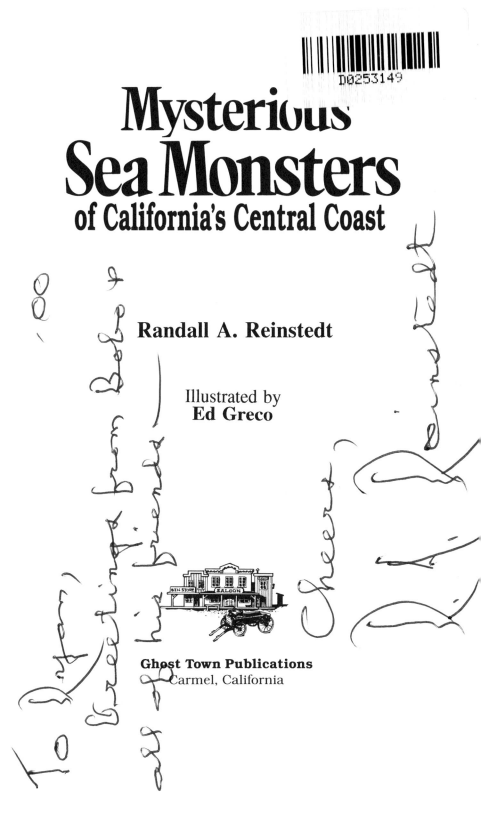

Ghost Town Publications
Carmel, California

If bookstores in your area do not carry *Mysterious Sea Monsters of California's Central Coast,* copies may be obtained by writing to . . .

GHOST TOWN PUBLICATIONS
P.O. Drawer 5998
Carmel, CA 93921

For other books by Randall A. Reinstedt see page 73.

This book is a revised and expanded version of the work by the same title originally published in 1979.

10 9 8 7 6 5 4 3 2

Manufactured in the United States of America

Library of Congress Catalog Number 80-114610
ISBN 0-933818-06-8

Edited by John Bergez
Typesetting and design by Erick and Mary Ann Reinstedt

About the cover: "Fisherman's Nightmare," by Ed Greco, was commissioned especially for this book. Although the "monster" it depicts is truly the stuff of nightmares, many a wary California fisherman has set out to sea chastened by tales of real-life encounters with strange and sometimes frightening denizens of the deep.

This book is dedicated to Monterey's men of the sea . . .
whose tales made this work possible

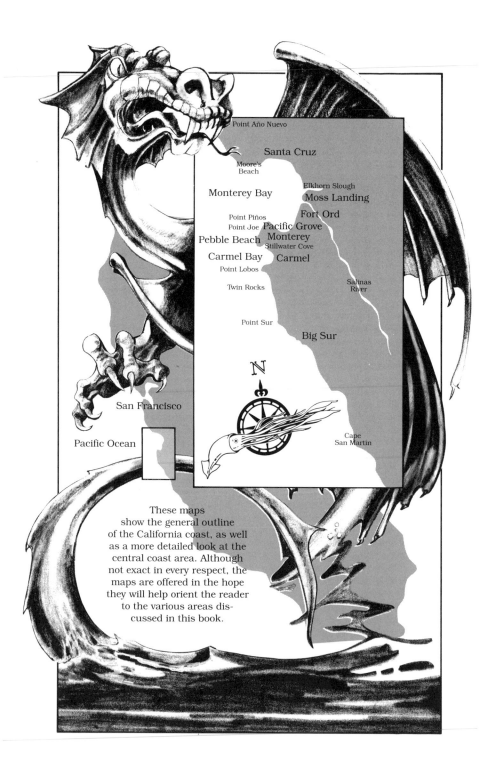

Point Año Nuevo

Santa Cruz

Moore's
Beach

Monterey Bay

Elkhorn Slough

Moss Landing

Point Piños

Fort Ord

Point Joe

Pacific Grove

Pebble Beach

Monterey

Stillwater Cove

Carmel Bay

Carmel

Point Lobos

Twin Rocks

Salinas
River

Point Sur

Big Sur

N

San Francisco

Cape
San Martin

Pacific Ocean

These maps
show the general outline
of the California coast, as well
as a more detailed look at the
central coast area. Although
not exact in every respect, the
maps are offered in the hope
they will help orient the reader
to the various areas dis-
cussed in this book.

Contents

Introduction

In 1975 I published a book called *Shipwrecks and Sea Monsters of California's Central Coast*. The book was well received and created considerable interest in shipwrecks in and around Monterey Bay. It also started people talking about the many strange creatures that inhabit these waters and the awesome submarine canyon that is at the bottom of the bay. This new interest in creatures of the deep, combined with repeated requests for more information about the odd assortment of sea beasts that have been spotted off our shores, prompted me to write an expanded version of the book's sea monster section. Published in 1979, this work was called *Mysterious Sea Monsters of California's Central Coast*. Even though the book was popular with sea monster buffs, after the first printing sold out I chose not to have it reprinted. Instead, I let the shipwreck book's sea monster section fill the void, as it answered most of the commonly asked questions and continued to stimulate people's interest in Monterey Bay's multitude of sea beasts and its vast submarine canyon.

In 1992, more than a dozen years after *Mysterious Sea Monsters* was published, I decided that the time had come to rewrite and expand it. This decision was arrived at for several reasons, not the least of which was the tremendous success of the Monterey Bay Aquarium. With the opening of this world-class facility in 1984, the marine life of Monterey Bay, and the study of its immense canyon, has become a subject of international interest.

Drawing millions of visitors to Monterey's historic Cannery Row, the Monterey Bay Aquarium has not only been a boon to the local economy but has created a new need for a book of this type. Unique in many ways, the aquarium has enabled people from far and near to thrill to the wonders of life in the sea. Also, the magnificent look at our underwater world that this facility affords has prompted countless questions and stimulated an ever-increasing interest in Monterey Bay, its king-sized canyon, and the marine life it harbors.

The decision to update and expand my original sea monster book was also influenced by the designation of Monterey Bay as a federal marine sanctuary in 1992. Thanks to the interest and hard work of thousands of people, what began as a dream in the 1970s is now a reality. When the official documents were finally signed, the Monterey Bay National Marine Sanctuary became the largest such refuge in the nation. Covering 5,312 square miles, it extends for 200 miles along the California coast. In the heart of this immense refuge is Monterey Bay, and at the bay's bottom is its famous submarine canyon (also known as the Monterey Trench). To most observers, this fathomless canyon is the focal point of the sanctuary, in part because its importance to scientists who study life in the sea is perhaps unequalled. In backing up this boast, the comments of a renowned marine researcher may be of interest. Speaking at a sanctuary dedication gathering in September 1992, the researcher said, "The canyon has more biological diversity per square centimeter, or mile, than the richest habitat on earth, including the rain forest."

With Monterey Bay alone harboring more than 340 kinds of fish, and at least 30 kinds of marine mammals (including sea otters, dolphins, whales, seals, sea lions, and porpoises), the sanctuary is indeed a rich resource. Add to this the fact that the Monterey Bay area is one of

California's most beautiful places to visit, and it is not difficult to see why the Monterey Peninsula, and its adjacent Big Sur coast, are among the Golden State's most popular tourist attractions. (Those who are interested in birds may wish to note that the Monterey Bay area is also special for them. In fact—at one place, at one time—116 species were counted! At the time this sighting was made, it was a world's record.)

With the vast amount of publicity the marine sanctuary has received, combined with the ongoing discoveries of unusual creatures of the deep by the Monterey Bay Aquarium (in cooperation with other research institutions), interest in the area's "sea monsters" has perhaps never been greater. I should also mention that in revising this work I had a certain group of people in mind. These individuals are the disbelievers—the people for whom the subject of sea monsters and newly discovered forms of marine life falls into the category of myth and legend. Sadly, many of the most stubborn skeptics have neglected to do their homework. In particular, the great majority have never availed themselves of the opportunity to track down the old-timers of Monterey's famed fishing fleet and listen to their astonishing accounts of the marine oddities they have seen with their own eyes.

The careers of the fishermen I speak of date back to the 1920s, 30s, and 40s, when Monterey was known as the Sardine Capital of the World. Today these men are in their 70s, 80s, and 90s. Even though they are getting along in years, many of these fishermen have vivid memories of their encounters with strange denizens of the deep. Anyone who takes the time to listen to the sagas these old-timers have to tell cannot easily discount their stories of "sea monsters."

But we do not have to rely on the tales of fisher-men—no matter how credible—to conclude that strange and still unexplained creatures lurk in California's coastal waters. To knowledgeable marine biologists, Monterey Bay is perhaps uniquely qualified to harbor unknown forms of marine life. The bay's submarine canyon—which plunges to *twice* the depth of the Grand Canyon—has been described as "one of the world's largest and least studied underwater chasms." Even today the mysteries of the Monterey Trench are only beginning to be explored with the aid of robot submarines and other new technology. And—despite the scoffing of the doubters—these explorations *are* turning up weird forms of animal life in the waters of the bay.

In August 1993, for example, marine scientists working with the Monterey Bay Aquarium Research Institute used a deep-sea diving device equipped with cameras and other special instruments to explore the dark waters nearly 800 feet below the surface of the bay. As reported in the *San Francisco Chronicle*, their space-age technology fished up a strange creature indeed—a type of jellyfish from the order Siphonophora. This particular siphonophore is actually an entire colony of separate beasts with many mouths and individual digestive tracts and reproductive organs. Each of its segments can even live independently for a short time. Although the tiny specimen caught by the institute's cameras was barely six inches long, one of the scientists pointed out that similar colonial creatures can reach 60 feet in length and boast 100 or more stomachs! He may have been joking when he referred to these amazing animals as "monster killers of the deep," but I think most of us would agree that a 60-foot collection of mouths and stomachs qualifies for that description!

Since it is now established that Monterey Bay is home to strange and unfamiliar sea beasts, isn't it also possible that fishermen of old did encounter bizarre forms of marine life? If so, how can we be sure that some of the creatures didn't resemble sea monsters in shape and size, just as the fishermen reported?

If you think such things could have occurred, and if you would like to learn more about such mysterious dwellers of the deep as Bobo (the legendary "Old Man of Monterey Bay"), this book is for you. So, make yourself comfortable—preferably overlooking the beautiful bay of Monterey—and settle in for some real-life tales about the creatures that have helped make this historic harbor such a remarkable place.

Acknowledgments

To acknowledge every person who has played a part in the preparation of this work would require a list of considerable length. With this in mind I would like to offer a general and heartfelt thanks to the many people who helped me along the way. I would especially like to thank my wife, Debbie, for supporting me in my decision to revise this book, and the Ghost Town Publications "team" for their interest and enthusiasm.

Perhaps even longer than a "people list" would be the list of sources that I consulted in tracking down information and confirming certain facts. However, even though I pored over countless publications in my quest for information, I would like to single out the *Monterey Peninsula Herald* newspaper for a special word of thanks. Over the years this source has furnished an abundance of information about Monterey Bay and the many creatures that frequent it.

In discussing valuable sources, and thinking back to my years of collecting information, I would be remiss not to acknowledge the fishermen of Monterey's famed sardine industry. Without these men who put Monterey on the map as a major fishing port, the number of local creature sightings would be considerably fewer. Sadly, many members of this fishing fraternity have departed our earthly waters and gone on to more plentiful fishing grounds. Still, as we go to press many of Monterey's aged fishermen are still part of the local scene. Those who have the good fortune of talking to them will learn that in many cases their memories of encounters with an odd assortment of sea beasts are as vivid today as they were on the day of their unique adventures.

In closing, I would like to dedicate this book to these men of the sea, and to those who have gone before. Without their accounts, and their generosity in sharing them, this work would not have been possible.

Chapter 1

GIANTS OF THE DEEP

Stories of encounters with frightening monsters and snake-like sea serpents have circulated throughout the Monterey Bay area for countless years. Unfortunately, as is the case with most such sagas, very few pictures have ever been taken of these elusive creatures of the deep. With a lack of pictures to document the sightings, most tales of Monterey Bay monsters are looked upon as nothing more than nautical nightmares or the figments of someone's overactive imagination.

However, before we scoff too long and too loudly at the multitude of stories and sightings, we should realize that if creatures of the deep are prone to venture close to shore (seeking food or a more hospitable environment, or perhaps out of sheer curiosity), the bay of Monterey must be considered an ideal haven for such maritime oddities.

To many people it comes as a surprise that Monterey Bay boasts the deepest underwater trench in North America. As I mentioned in the Introduction, the Monterey Submarine Canyon drops to twice the depth of Arizona's Grand Canyon. From the floor of the bay the trench extends far out into the Pacific Ocean. Through the research facilities of the Monterey Bay Aquarium, along with a growing number of other institutions, we are learning more about what does—and doesn't—exist in this underwater world. Considering that this great abyss has not been fully explored, and that previously unknown life forms have already been found, we do not have to stretch our imaginations far to conjure up a vast assortment of snake-like serpents and multiarmed monsters that *might* inhabit this awesome trench.

Another favorite hiding place for the monsters of Monterey Bay was said to have been at the mouth of the Salinas River, where old-timers claim a "bottomless pit" was located. A little research will disclose that the old-timers' tales have circulated throughout the Monterey Bay area for countless years, but what is less clear is *which* Salinas River mouth the stories are talking about.

Most long-time Monterey Bay residents know that the Salinas River's original outlet was through Elkhorn Slough (north of the present-day Salinas River mouth), which meets the sea at the bayside community of Moss Landing, on Monterey Bay's east shore. In following this point of local history one step further, it is of interest to note that Monterey Bay's submarine canyon is said by some to be the natural continuation of the Elkhorn Slough/Salinas River channels. With this thought in mind, I can't help but wonder whether the bottomless pit referred to in old legends is the same submarine canyon that scientists now describe as harboring a vast assortment of strange and unusual creatures of the deep.

The multitude of stories and legends of Monterey Bay area "sea monsters" includes any number of accounts of multi-humped serpents and snake-like sea beasts—creatures similar in description to various maritime oddities that are part of the folklore of many seafaring nations. The great majority of these accounts are undoubtedly nothing more than fantasies, or cases of mistaken identity of such creatures as the enormous blue whale, the grotesque giant squid, the snake-like oarfish, or the evil-appearing octopus.

Of course, exaggerated tales originally told to frighten or impress are also often accepted as fact by a surprising number of gullible listeners and are soon being retold as documented accounts.

But does this mean that *all* the tales of strange and often frightening sea beasts can be dismissed as instances of mistaken identity or fictionalized dreams? Or do mysterious and still uncatalogued "monsters" inhabit the depths of California's coastal waters? Perhaps an example or two of well-documented specimens will give the doubters pause . . .

One of the best examples of odd—and enormous—creatures that have been proven to lurk in our oceans came to light in a story that began approximately 100 years ago, in 1896. As strange as it seems, the final chapter of this fascinating tale was not recorded until 1971!

The account begins on a St. Augustine, Florida, beach, where the remains of a partially decomposed beast were cast upon the shore. Even though the remains were studied by numerous people, the identity of the creature remained a mystery until marine biologist A. E. Verrill identified the 12,000-pound hulk as a giant octopus! Appropriately dubbed *Octopus giganteus verrill,* this granddaddy of all octopi became the talk of the Florida coast.

Inasmuch as this awesome beast would have been a true monster—10 to 15 times larger than any previously known octopus—Verrill's identification was soon questioned by the astounded public, as well as by fellow scientists. Finding himself alone in his conviction, and ridiculed by other marine biologists, Verrill decided that he might have been a bit hasty in making his identification. The beleaguered biologist then announced that the decomposed carcass was "probably" that of a whale instead.

The public greeted this announcement with understandable enthusiasm, as they now had renewed assurance that there were no multiarmed monsters of gigantic proportions lurking on the ocean floor. After Verrill's change of mind, the matter was no longer considered newsworthy and was soon forgotten.

Three quarters of a century passed before Verrill's *Octopus giganteus* again made the news. The year was 1971, and the place was the Smithsonian Institution in Washington, D.C. Two marine biologists, using advanced scientific techniques, were able to examine a slice of the creature that had washed up on the Florida beach so many years before. Fortunately, a portion of Verrill's mystery monster had been preserved in alcohol and stored at the institution. With the use of a special polarized light source, the two scientists reexamined the aged creature and found—to everyone's surprise—that its tissue structure *was* that of an octopus after all! According to their findings, the multiarmed beast would have stretched a distance of 200 feet—two-thirds the length of a football field!

While not nearly as startling as Verrill's long-ago find, closer to home a "monster" of more modest proportions was discovered in the waters of Monterey Bay. According to the 1975 *Guinness Book of World Records*, "The largest known octopus is the common Pacific octopus (*Octopus apollyon*). One specimen trapped in a fisherman's net in Monterey Bay, California, had a radial spread of over 20 feet and scaled 110 lbs." While only one-tenth the estimated span of the Florida beast, this Monterey Bay monster was large enough to embrace a two-story building. Who is to say there are not octopi of even larger proportions lurking to this day in Monterey's rounded bay?

Another example of quite a stir created by an oversized creature from the sea was the catch of a giant eel larva by a research ship from the country of Denmark. The larva was so large that, judging from larvae of other species, the mature eel would have reached a length of 90 feet! Since no eels of this size had ever been caught, a second research vessel was dispatched with hopes of capturing a full-grown specimen. Probing the ocean depths at the 1,200-foot level, the vessel managed to get hold of *something* . . . only to have the unknown creature bend a three-foot iron hook and escape! To this day scientists are puzzled over just what that "something" was that straightened the hook.

Dropping even deeper we find the giant squid. Considered by some to be the most terrifying of all living things, this evil-appearing creature has been the basis for numerous sea monster sagas. Among these tales are accounts of the multiarmed monster of Norwegian folklore known as the kraken that date back hundreds of years.

In looking more closely at the deep-dwelling squid, we find the term "giant" to be fitting indeed. The largest of these ink-emitting, 10-tentacled creatures that has ever been officially recorded stretched almost 60 feet in length—as long as 10 average-sized men laid end to end! Estimated to have weighed more than 8,000 pounds when alive, it was a true monster of the deep. In addition to this documented nautical nightmare, there have been unconfirmed reports from various parts of the world of squid-like creatures stretching up to 100 feet in length. A little more food for thought is provided by one of the world's leading experts on such matters, who believes that there are adult giant squid in our oceans that measure between 100 and 150 feet!

While we're discussing creatures in excess of 100 feet, we mustn't forget about the jellyfish. Granted, the gentle-seeming jellyfish doesn't usually come to mind when we think about monsters of the sea. However, in 1865 a specimen measuring 245 feet from fringe to fringe is said to have washed ashore on New England's Cape Ann. If this account is true, we must add the jellyfish to our sea monster Hall of Fame, as the Cape Ann specimen would be the longest creature ever recorded—on land *or* sea!

In continuing our discussion of king-sized creatures of the deep, it should be mentioned that at a depth of about 3,000 feet (perhaps twice the depth of the giant squid) reports indicate an object of unknown shape and size has been scientifically recorded. Detected by explosive sonic means, the object—for lack of a better name—was simply listed as a "sizable something." With scientific proof that an object of unknown origin and apparently huge size does exist more than half a mile below the surface of the sea, we must admit that scientists still have much to learn about the possibly gigantic inhabitants of the ocean depths.

With a "sizable something" at about the 3,000-foot level, and with certain sections of the Monterey Canyon dropping to more than three times that depth, one can't help but wonder what enormous creatures might be lurking in the dark crevices of this vast trench. With approximately two miles of water between the deepest parts of the canyon and the surface water of the Pacific, there is certainly more than enough room for beasts of immense size to live their entire lives without being seen.

Interestingly, the biggest creature that *has* been seen in local waters is none other than the largest mammal ever to have inhabited the earth—the great blue whale. The largest of the blues reach a length of about 100 feet, and weigh approximately 300,000 pounds. Inshore visits by these behemoths are relatively rare, with scientists suspecting that their periodic stopovers in Monterey Bay are partly due to the food supply generated by the trench.

With whales in the 100- to 150-ton category occasionally visiting Monterey Bay, it must be admitted that our local waters *do* harbor gigantic creatures of the deep. Fortunately, these peace-loving creatures do not have the killer instinct and, instead of devouring anything that comes within range, they feed almost entirely on plankton (small sea animals and plants). The largest and fastest of the whale family, these mammoth monsters also happen to be toothless!

Several other species of whale also frequent the waters of Monterey Bay, including the deadly killer whale. Reaching a length of 30 feet, killer whales hunt in packs and have been known to gang up on their 100-ton cousins and slaughter them mercilessly. With an abundance of very large and very sharp teeth in their powerful jaws, killer whales will attack anything within reach in their search for food. In the stomach of one relatively small killer whale (14 feet in length), the remains of 13 porpoises and 14 seals were found—quite the opposite of the dainty diet consumed by his oversized cousin, the great blue.

Whales bigger than dinosaurs, cunning killers of the sea that hunt in packs—these marvels seem commonplace only because their existence has been well documented. I wonder what our reaction would be if, like people in ancient times, we had never seen the proof that such creatures inhabited our oceans. Would we dismiss the tales of sailors and fishermen as legend and fantasy?

Chapter 2

THE OLD MAN
OF MONTEREY BAY

In addition to the killer whales and the great blues, an assortment of other denizens of the deep inhabit or visit the waters of Monterey Bay, including various other whale species and several types of shark (such as the rare sleeper shark that was brought up from the 2,200-foot depths of the Monterey Trench in 1974). Of course, these relatively common inhabitants of the deep—regardless of how large and ferocious they may be—are not usually tagged with the name "sea monster." To most people a sea monster is a seldom-seen something, usually quite grotesque in appearance, that upon occasion will rise from the water and scare the daylights out of anyone who has the misfortune of seeing it.

While there are a multitude of sea creatures that might fit this definition, the famed "Old Man of Monterey Bay" perhaps fits better than most. Having been sighted by numerous people over a period of many years, this mysterious monster—better known as Bobo to most local residents—has become a Monterey Bay area legend. (How Bobo may have gotten his name is discussed later in this chapter.)

While the majority of sightings of this strange creature date back to the heyday of Monterey's sardine industry, other reports—both before and after the prosperous years of the sardine—have also been recorded. Sighted in various parts of the bay and along the Monterey County coast, the creature was most often seen in the early mornings or in the dusk of early evening. It has been described in various ways over the years, but the majority of the reports describe the "Old Man" as having a long, thin, snake-like body (although there are those who swear it was shaped more like a sea elephant) and boasting an evil-appearing, human-like head or face. The length of the creature has been reported as anywhere from 15 to 150 feet, with at least one newspaper account describing it as being even longer!

Monterey's veteran sardine fishermen often describe the Old Man of Monterey Bay as being "as long as a telephone pole, but much wider." How much wider is open to question. Most old-timers hesitate to guess its width because all they usually saw of it was its neck and head, with an occasional glimpse of a hump or two along its slender, snake-like body. Descriptions of the coloring of the body also vary, with the majority of opinions seeming to agree that it was on the dark side. The tail of the beast has rarely been described. The most detailed description of the tail on record states: "It was very sharp, tapered, and had the smallest rudder fins for a body of such size that can be imagined. On the underside of the tail there appeared to be vacuum cups similar to those of octopus tentacles."

Accounts of the startling human-like qualities of the head come from Monterey fishermen of the 1920s, 30s, and 40s, as it was they who most often spotted the creature. To this day many of these pioneer fishermen will tell in detail, with animated gestures and a lingering sense of awe, of their encounters with the Old Man of Monterey Bay. It would probably not take too many discussions with these respected old-timers to convince even the hardiest skeptics that there is truth to their tales. As you read the following accounts, imagine them as they were told to me, with earnest conviction, by the veterans of Monterey's famed sardine fleet . . .

Spotted quite frequently over a 20-year period, the Old Man of Monterey Bay (or, simply, Bobo) was a favorite topic of conversation among the crew members of Monterey's purse seiners, or sardine boats. Upon occasion the mysterious monster would be seen by the entire crew of a 12-man boat. Telling how the creature would suddenly surface in the choppy waters of the bay, the dumbfounded fishermen often described the mournful look on the creature's face and the large, baleful eyes that stared at the vessel and the men aboard. Rising and falling in the water, the long slender neck and rounded head were at times said to reach a height of 12 feet! Even though the mournful look and the baleful eyes were frequently described, detailed descriptions of the face are hard to come by, as the creature was seldom seen at close range.

One sighting that *was* made at extremely close range—and was reported in detail in Monterey and San Francisco newspapers (and who knows how many others)—gives credibility to the many reports of an evil-eyed monster lurking in local waters, as well as to other accounts described in this book. Taking place in 1938, the sighting was described in a *Monterey Peninsula Herald* article that boasted the headline " 'Old Man Of Bay' Back On Top—Weird Monster Sighted Again." The following story goes on to say that all aboard the purse seiner *Dante Allighieri* viewed the huge beast as they were making a run across Monterey Bay (heading in the direction of Santa Cruz on the bay's north shore).

According to the newspaper account, the vessel was approximately 75 minutes out of Monterey and passing over the deepest part of the bay's submarine canyon when one of the crew spotted "what appeared to be a huge white human face." The man shouted for his shipmates to "look!" and in a matter of seconds the entire crew stood gawking at the four-foot-wide face.

As the boat drifted to within "boat-hook distance" of the creature, its eyes were closed and it appeared to be taking a midday nap. Suddenly, as if sensing their presence, the man-like monster awoke with a snort and flashed coal-black eyes at the crew. Apparently frightened by the gawking fishermen and the nearness of the vessel, the creature again snorted and dug its two fins in the water as it rolled over and dived.

With the "Old Man" gone, the crew could only speak in awe of their startling experience and make the captain—a veteran of three such sightings—promise to get a camera and keep it on board.

In the absence of pictures, all we have are the verbal accounts given by the *Dante Allighieri's* crew. The body of the creature was described as being "30-odd feet" in length and ending in a fish-like tail. The best overall description of the frightening beast was provided by the crew member who made the original sighting. This man was quoted in the *Herald* as saying that the creature had "a very old man's or monkey's face, with eyes twice the diameter of breakfast buns, and a mouth like a crescent moon. Barnacles were all over the head, and also along the black body. Folds of white skin hung beneath the neck. The body was as big around as a pick-up truck. It must have weighed maybe eight or nine tons."

This information was enough to convince at least a few skeptics that something strange did indeed inhabit the waters of Monterey Bay. As reporter Winsor Josselyn stated

in closing his front-page account more than 50 years ago, "Monterey has its own sea monster right here in its own front yard."

The close-up encounter of the *Dante Allighieri* was only one of many Bobo sightings. Even though many of the fishermen who saw the beast agreed that the face of Monterey Bay's mysterious "Old Man" had human-like qualities to it, there were those who disagreed and described the monster's head in various other ways. Some said it was bull-like, with long, sloping shoulders, while others likened its appearance to that of a crocodile, giraffe, elephant, horse, serpent, or duck.

After the human-like descriptions, the crocodile likenesses seemed to rank second in popularity. For some reason, the majority of the "crocodile-like" sightings were reported by people who observed the creature from shore. In the late 1940s there was a rash of such sightings in the Pacific Grove, Monterey, and Fort Ord areas. Almost to a person, witnesses who made sightings from shore described the creature as extremely long, approximately four feet in diameter, and multi-humped. Reports of the coloring indicated that the body was either tan or gray. The serpent-like head was said to have been flat in appearance, with eyes like those of an African crocodile. The teeth were described as being V-shaped and in an even line, much like the teeth of a saw.

Another interesting sighting made from shore was of a "critter" that the witness described as resembling a giraffe. The sighting took place in the early 1930s and was made by a lad who was then 14. Today this respected Monterey man remembers the event vividly, even though it took place approximately 60 years ago.

On his way home from school late one afternoon, the teenage boy was walking along the railroad tracks near the Booth Cannery (today the site is near Monterey's Heritage Harbor complex). Upon looking toward the breakwater, which was then under construction, the lad was shocked to see a long, slender neck—topped by a giraffe-like head—suddenly rise from the water! Too surprised to speak, the young Montereyan stared at the creature as it looked from side to side. Apparently satisfied—or perhaps terrified—at what it saw, the giraffe-like giant "almost immediately" dropped its head back in the water. While this was taking place, the shocked teenager managed to regain his voice and shout for his friends to look. Unfortunately, as they stared in the direction their awestruck companion pointed, all that was left for them to see was a churned-up wake as the creature swam "with terrific speed" toward the one-mile buoy off the north end of Cannery Row.

In a conversation with the Monterey man who made this sighting, the following facts were brought to light: The creature was within, and slightly to the south, of what then existed of the breakwater, which makes this incident the only *known* sighting of an unidentifiable sea beast within the confines of the breakwater. The weather was clear and the sea was calm when the incident occurred. The creature was approximately 200 yards from shore when it was sighted. The head was comparatively small and appeared to stick out of the water approximately 12 feet. Finally, in describing the neck, the Montereyan told how it appeared to be tapered and how it rose and fell as if it were "levered" (similar to the way a man's arm would bend toward his body from the elbow, with the fist acting as the head).

With these details adding an air of authenticity to the tale, this rare harbor sighting of a giraffe-like giant of the deep takes on added meaning. Whatever the explanation may be, I believe the tale should be accepted by sea serpent searchers as an important chapter in the continuing saga of mysterious monsters of Monterey Bay.

In addition to stories of sea creatures resembling a crocodile or giraffe, there are a number of accounts of local sea beasts resembling an elephant. Records indicate that shore parties and fishermen alike reported seeing such trunk-faced behemoths. The majority of the sightings took place in the vicinity of the present-day Salinas River mouth, near the entrance to Moss Landing's Elkhorn Slough.

For unknown reasons, the elephant-like monster was most often spotted during times of heavy fog. The following description (credited to an early Monterey fisherman) is thought to be one of the most detailed of the numerous accounts that were given of this elephant-faced creature:

> He had an odd elephant-like trunk that he would inflate and make terrifying noises with. Large reddish eyes protruded from each side of its head, which seemed to stare with an evil glow about them. Its snake-like body rose from the water, and small arm-like fins beat at the air as if it was using them to help keep its balance.

As exaggerated as this likeness may sound, it was told in sober seriousness, and the sighting was very real to the man who made it. In checking similar sightings in and around Monterey Bay, one soon discovers that even though descriptions of the body varied, those of the face were remarkably consistent. In an attempt to place this red-eyed monster in the realm of reality, local marine biologists were consulted. The outcome was a somewhat scientific explanation of what Monterey Bay's elephant-like sea beast may have been.

According to these experts—whose conclusions are supported by books about creatures of the deep—Monterey's mysterious trunked-faced sea monster may have been nothing more than an elephant seal, a marine mammal that was somewhat rare in Monterey Bay waters during the days of the sardine. In elaborating on this explanation, the marine biologists told how elephant seals dive to great depths and have large, glowing eyes. The males of the species boast an elephant-like trunk, and can grow to monstrous proportions with some adult males tipping the scales at nearly three tons!

With such thoughts in mind, and with a tip of the hat to our local research scientists, it may be safe to assume that Monterey Bay's elephant-like sea monster was nothing more than a misplaced elephant seal that found its way to our rounded bay. In this connection, it is of interest to note that since the early days of local monster sightings elephant seals have become more common along the Monterey and Santa Cruz County coasts. In fact, Point Ano Nuevo, slightly north of the Santa Cruz County line, is today a California State Reserve—and a breeding ground for elephant seals. The reserve is the only known spot where the northern elephant seal regularly visits the mainland.

Carrying the story of elephant-like sea creatures one step further, a newspaper account dating from the late 1940s quotes a respected local marine scientist as indicating he thought the "serpent with an ape-like head" that had been spotted in Monterey waters was a sea elephant with a mussel-like sea animal attached to its face. Just how this could have taken place was not elaborated upon, but if such an event did occur it is certainly not difficult to imagine the nightmarish-appearing creature that would have resulted!

As I noted earlier in this chapter, "elephant-like" was one of the many descriptions applied to Monterey's most famous sea monster, the legendary Bobo. Why this creature was blessed with such an unmonster-like name is open to question. Perhaps, as some old-timers suggest, the name was borrowed from its "monster cousin" of the Cape San Martin area, approximately 60 miles south of Monterey. Even though these California sea monsters boasted the same name and apparently lived relatively close to each other, they were not identical in appearance. While the Bobo of the Monterey Bay area (particularly the Bobo of late 1940s vintage) was often described as elephant-like in appearance, the Bobo of Cape San Martin was frequently described as having a face that resembled a giant gorilla! Observed by numerous residents of south Monterey County in the 1930s and 40s, the Cape San Martin monster was discussed in numerous publications, including the authoritative sea monster book *In the Wake of the Sea Serpents* by Bernard Heuvelmans.

There is a second tale concerning how Monterey Bay's Bobo was "tagged with a brand," however—one that takes us back more than 60 years. It was told to me by a man who has lived in Monterey for approximately three quarters of a century. The tale is important to the history of the area both because it explains how Bobo may have been named and because it reminds us once again that strange creatures have been sighted in Monterey waters for longer than most people can remember.

To appreciate the story it is of interest to know that in the early 1900s Monterey's fishing industry was represented by a variety of nationalities. Although Italian fishermen were the most numerous, the following tale was told to me by an Oriental gentleman, who had learned it from a fellow of Portuguese descent.

The story goes like this. One day during the 1920s, a lone Portuguese fisherman frantically rowed his one-man boat to the Monterey wharf. The man was both frightened and exhausted as he tied up his boat and climbed to the main level of the pier. Upon reaching a gathering of his friends, the wide-eyed fisherman began telling them of a terrifying encounter he had had with an odd-looking creature in the bay.

Even though it was obvious that the man was genuinely shaken, his waterfront friends proceeded to make fun of him. They laughed as the terror-stricken fisherman tried to describe the beast he had seen. Teasing him, they called him names and told him to "quit acting like a bobo!" (In Portuguese, *bobo* means such things as a fool or a dunce.)

For a number of years after this incident took place, many fishermen refused to talk about their experiences when they saw a sea beast they were unable to identify. They were sure they would be teased—and called "a bobo." From that time on, it is said, the Old Man of Monterey Bay was frequently referred to as Bobo the Sea Monster—or just plain Bobo!

Chapter 3

SEA ELEPHANTS OR
SEA MONSTERS?

The area of the Monterey Peninsula coastline between Monterey Bay and the scenic village of Carmel is noted for several picturesque promontories. One such headland is Point Joe, named after a squatter who lived there for many years. In addition to its rugged beauty and pyramid-shaped rocks, this outcropping of land is also known for the ships that have come to grief there—particularly the *St. Paul* in 1896—and the conflicting currents that meet off its craggy shore. In a westerly direction from this treacherous point, at a place old-time fishermen refer to as Codfish Bank, the sighting of a mysterious sea creature was made in September 1930. With varying reports and descriptions coming from different members of the purse seiner crew who made the sighting, perhaps the only safe thing to say is that something quite large—and difficult to identify—was spotted on that long-ago day.

One aged fisherman, who was a crew member at the time and who has fished in Monterey waters for over 50 years, told me the creature had a neck that was three to four feet across. The beast's body was "sort of peaked," he reported, and its head was slightly smaller than its neck. Most startling of all, from a distance of 70 to 80 feet, which was as close as the vessel was able to get, the creature

29

looked "like an enormous human being"! Not only did its body (at least the portion that appeared above water) look "almost human," but its head and face also had human-like qualities—except for its huge, protruding eyes.

At the time of the sighting, between 10:00 and 11:00 a.m., the sea was calm and the weather was clear. When the beast was first spotted, it appeared to be eyeing the vessel and the men aboard it. As it continued to bob in the water, the creature's human-like head and brownish body rose to a height of approximately six feet. As the boat slowly continued its approach, the "Codfish Bank beast" took one last look at the vessel and the gaping crew members who lined its rail. Then it unceremoniously sank from sight.

Interestingly, before the creature was totally lost from view, my fisherman friend climbed the boat's mast to get a better look. From this vantage point, he said, he could see the beast after it submerged. Fortunately for this account—and for my quick-thinking friend—the creature chose to swim toward the vessel, passing directly underneath it at a depth of 20 to 30 feet. With the sun brightly shining, the fisherman was able to get a comparatively clear look at the beast as it passed under the boat. As strange as it seems in light of the "human-like" qualities previously described, the fisherman stated that the creature had fins and an enormous tail like that of a sea lion. Seen from the mast, the creature with the man-like head looked for all the world like a beast of the sea elephant variety!

While it might be tempting to conclude that the mysterious beast in the preceding account was nothing more than an elephant seal or similar creature, that does not

31

explain its uncanny human-like appearance above the water. In this connection a second account is of interest at this point. This tale may make sea monster buffs think twice before bunching the many unexplained beasts of the Monterey Bay area into the sea elephant/elephant seal category.

The story was told to me by a native Montereyan who, along with his family, has been part of the local fishing scene for much of this century. In July 1948, the tale goes, a creature was spotted by the crew members of a fishing boat at "mid-bay," directly over the Monterey Trench. The sighting occurred at daybreak (approximately 6:00 a.m.). When first seen, the beast was between 150 and 175 yards from the 55-foot boat. As the vessel drifted closer, the creature bobbed in the water "like a buoy" and was observed by all nine members of the crew. The beast was dark in color and rose to a height of between four and six feet above the water.

According to my fisherman informant, the creature's upper body looked "cone-shaped" and was approximately four feet wide. The head was only slightly narrower than the body and appeared to sit squarely on top of the creature's sloping shoulders without the support of a neck, or else resting on a very thick one. The face resembled a person, with a flat nose and large, blinking eyes. Other facial features that made this beast unique included a black "Chinaman-type" beard and mustache! Other than the beard and mustache, the body was void of hair.

Bobo, as the creature was called by the teller of this tale, did not appear to be frightened as the vessel approached. However, as is the case in two other accounts mentioned in this book, one of the fishermen grabbed the boat's rifle and took a shot at the beast. Although it wasn't hit, upon being fired at the creature immediately sank from sight.

Just why the crew member shot at the beast was not elaborated upon, but the vessel's captain—who had seen Bobo on several other occasions—let it be known that he was extremely angry with the fisherman who fired the shot.

In concluding his story the aged Montereyan mused a while about Bobo and what it was or was not. To this long-time fisherman, two facts were plain: Bobo was real, and it "was definitely *not* a sea elephant!"

As a follow-up to the preceding story, another Monterey Bay sighting comes to mind. Taking place in the early 1920s, the incident involved one of Monterey's most respected fishermen. Even though nearly 60 years had passed since the time of the sighting, this long-time Montereyan and former purse seiner captain remembered well his encounter with the mysterious creature.

As his account began, one day when he was still in his teens he made his way to the Monterey wharf and prepared his small boat for an outing. After checking his gear, he headed across the bay toward the community of Santa Cruz to troll for salmon. After several unsuccessful hours of fishing he decided to pull in his lines and return home. As he headed toward Monterey on that clear and calm day—passing over the Submarine Canyon in the process—he saw a peculiar-looking object floating in the water. Not knowing what to make of it, but noting that from a distance it resembled a person waving, he turned his vessel toward it to see if he could be of help. As he approached to within 50 yards of the object, he suddenly realized that instead of someone in trouble, he was looking at a huge sea beast!

Terrified at the thought of being alone, and over the trench with a strange creature of the deep, the frightened teen made a hasty exit from the area. Not looking back as he frantically sought the shelter of the Monterey harbor, the young fisherman thought "horrible thoughts" and kept his eyes glued to the distant shore. Uppermost in his mind were the stories he had heard about men and boats (and other assorted objects) that had disappeared without a trace from the waters of Monterey Bay. Thinking that the beast he had just encountered might be responsible for those disappearances, the frantic lad managed to coax a little more life into his vessel's engine and raced toward the safety of the Monterey wharf.

Upon finally reaching the friendly waters of the Monterey harbor, and realizing he had safely outrun the king-sized creature, he thought long and hard about what he had seen. It was then that he realized how difficult it would be to describe the beast. With this in mind, and knowing that because of his age and lack of experience he was sure to be teased, he decided to keep the story to himself. It wasn't until Bobo sightings became much more common, and were accepted as fact by many members of Monterey's fishing fraternity, that the teller of this tale disclosed his frightening encounter with the Old Man of Monterey Bay.

When I interviewed this gentleman in 1979 and asked for a description of the creature, the aged fisherman explained that when he realized it was huge—and alive—he didn't wait around to look for details! Upon further questioning he did say that the beast was "brownish" in color and "barrel-like" in appearance. When I asked if the object could have been a creature of the sea elephant or elephant seal variety, he answered with an emphatic "No!" Almost as an afterthought, this popular ex-skipper went on to say that he had seen such beasts many times, and what he saw on that long-ago day did not have a trunk and definitely did not resemble a creature of the sea elephant family.

Another Monterey Bay sighting made by one of the local fishing fraternity's better-known personalities took place in either 1939 or 1940. In sharing his account with me this former sardine-boat captain described the beast in considerable detail. From a distance, he said, the creature reminded him and his 10-man crew of an "old-time hard-hat diver, complete with diving suit!" As their vessel approached to within 30 yards of the beast, its face appeared to have two large "old man's" eyes. Above the eyes were bump-like "coils" that "pulsated" as if it was breathing through them. Unfortunately, with his attention having been focused on the creature's pulsating coils and human-like eyes, the ex-skipper couldn't remember what its nose or mouth looked like.

As the boat circled the beast—with the crew taking care not to get too close—the creature turned in the water and followed it with its eyes. All the while it bobbed in the sea, rising to a height of approximately four feet. Its body was estimated to be about a yard wide and was gray-brown in color. Its neck and head appeared "as one" and were void of hair. After about 10 minutes the beast dropped from sight.

Interestingly, before the creature sank into the water the ex-captain indicated he had considered laying a net around it. However, he decided against this idea because he didn't know how long the creature was, and he didn't want to risk ruining the net.

As with other accounts, the ex-skipper stated that one of his crew had grabbed the vessel's gun and was about to

35

shoot the beast. Luckily, he was able to stop him before he pulled the trigger.

A few added facts shared by this long-time fisherman indicated that the sighting—as so often seems to have been the case—was made above the Monterey Trench. The water at that point dropped to a depth of "at least 200 fathoms" (1,200 feet), which was the maximum depth that could be recorded on the purse seiner's fathom meter. How much deeper the canyon might have been at the point where the sighting was made, the ex-skipper could not say.

In continuing with his story, the ex-captain related that after seeing the creature he bought a camera to keep on board the boat. Unfortunately, he never saw "Bobo" (as he called the beast) again.

Sea elephants or sea monsters? While there will always be those who prefer to believe that only those creatures already documented by science can exist in our local waters, the sheer number of strange sightings by sober and respected men of the sea must surely make us pause and wonder. Adding to the credibility of these accounts is the fact that so many of the sightings have occurred over, or near, the unexplored depths of Monterey Bay's Submarine Canyon. But until some future adventurer—whether fisherman or scientist—supplies documentary proof, the legendary beasts of Monterey Bay, like the dark canyon itself, will remain shrouded in mystery.

Chapter 4

THE WHITE-HAIRED SEA BEAST OF THE BIG SUR COAST

About 25 miles south of the Monterey Peninsula lies the rugged coast of Big Sur, an area that is world-renowned for its scenic beauty. But if the following tale is any indication, this spectacular stretch of California coastline may harbor natural wonders that are much less well known, and no less astonishing, than its staggering vistas.

The incident, as related to me by one of the fishermen who experienced it, took place approximately 12 miles west of the Big Sur coast. It was on a sunny summer morning in the late 1940s when the three-man crew of a Monterey-based albacore boat saw a strange object floating in the water. Seen from a distance of approximately 150 yards, the object appeared to be part of a small, white, half-sunken boat. The curious fishermen cut their engine and allowed their boat to drift toward the "abandoned vessel," pulling in their fishing lines as they went. Peering at the water, the crew soon realized that what they were approaching was definitely *not* the remains of a boat!

As they drifted closer to the mysterious object, the fishermen saw that the "white" they had mistakenly identified as part of a vessel was actually long, flowing white hair! Seeing a mass of white hair floating in the Pacific was startling enough, but amazement gave way to fright as the crew realized that the hair was attached to the head of a creature that was very much alive!

As the realization dawned that they were approaching a sizable sea beast, the fishermen's concern began to turn to panic. Frantically continuing to pull in their lines as they drifted ever closer to the creature, they saw that it appeared to be unaware of their presence and continued to loll in the calm water with its back to the boat. Suddenly, as if it was angry at being disturbed, the round-shouldered beast turned and stared at the boat and its terrified crew. Rising to a height of about 12 feet, the "monkey-faced" monster glared at the men through "saucer-shaped eyes" that the crew later said were approximately a foot wide! The creature's size and its glaring eyes were terrifying enough, but according to the teller of this tale its appearance was all the more ghastly because of its ape-like mouth and the evil grin on its face. "After what seemed like forever," the man went on, the creature appeared to tire of its visitors and sank below the surface, disappearing from sight.

In relating the details of his frightening experience, the Monterey man mentioned that he rarely discusses the incident with his fellow fishermen because they scoff at his story and think he is making it up. This comment recalls the experience of the lone Portuguese fisherman who, more than 60 years ago, was called a "bobo" after describing his encounter with a strange sea beast. With "monster scoffers" still very much in evidence among the fishing fraternity, who knows what additional stories never come to light because of the fear of ridicule?

In bringing this south coast saga to a close, the albacore fisherman went on to say that the creature's hair was "as white as snow" and that it "went up in the front—like a woman's—and down the back to what appeared to be the waist." The creature's skin was gray, and the monkey-like or ape-like face (similar in appearance to the more southerly

sightings of the Cape San Martin monster) had a wide nose with flat nostrils. According to the fisherman's father, who had seen the beast in the same area on a different occasion, the creature's tail resembled that of a fish. Perhaps most astonishing is the fisherman's description of ape-like arms and "what appeared to be hands" in the place of fins. These details make this Big Sur sighting unique among all the accounts of sea beasts along California's central coast—and perhaps anywhere in the world.

Another report involving albacore fishermen takes us from the waters off the Big Sur coast to an area closer to Monterey Bay. This incident took place in the fall of 1939 approximately nine miles southwest of the Point Pinos lighthouse, located at the southern tip of the bay.

The story was shared with me by a crew member of the albacore boat *Santa Anna*. Having fished in local waters for 45 years, the teller of this tale is a well-known and respected Monterey fisherman. As he related the incident in an upstairs room of an aged Monterey wharf warehouse, several of the man's friends gathered around. Unlike the "monster-scoffing" fishermen of previous tales, these veterans of the sea nodded in agreement as the man described the long-ago incident.

According to the fisherman's account, the *Santa Anna* was following a second vessel to the Monterey harbor when the lead boat suddenly swerved away from something bobbing in the sea. Curious as to what it was that was floating in the Pacific, the skipper of the *Santa Anna* cut his engine and allowed the boat to drift toward the mysterious object. The crew's first impression was that the object was nothing more than a log. As they closed in, however, they realized that the "log" was actually an odd-shaped creature that somewhat resembled a beast of the sea elephant or sea lion family.

Noiselessly the *Santa Anna* drifted to within a few feet of the creature, which seemed to be unaware of the vessel. Suddenly one member of the crew grabbed a gaff pole (used to land fish) and gave the strange creature a poke. Upon being jabbed, the slumbering sea beast awoke with a start, took one frantic look at the boat, and immediately sank into the sea.

Being a teenager at the time, and not accustomed to such adventures, the *Santa Anna* crew member who related this tale was, by his own account, considerably shaken by this close encounter. Decades later, he vividly recalled his fright and how he hid behind the fisherman who manned the gaff pole.

As he continued with his story, seeming to relive it as he spoke, the following facts were brought to light. The creature was spotted in the late afternoon, possibly between 4:00 and 5:00 p.m. It was bright and sunny when the sighting was made, and the water was "flat calm." There were four men aboard the *Santa Anna* when the incident took place. When the crew first sighted the floating object, it was approximately 500 to 600 yards away. The head, as they neared it, appeared to be about three feet in diameter and stuck out of the water between four and five feet. The face had a sea-elephant look to it, but the nose (or snout) was much smaller. The eyes were far apart on the sides of the head. When the creature opened them after being poked, they appeared to be "roundish and four to five inches across." The body was dark in color and had wrinkled skin. The facial skin was loose and in folds, "sort of like blubber." The body was similar in shape to a sea lion's, but according to the fisherman was "fifty times bigger than that of a sea elephant"! Seal-like fins appeared to be on each side of the body approximately six feet below the surface. The water in the area the sighting was made was estimated to have been a half-mile in depth.

What species of sea beast would such an odd creature have been? To this day, no one knows. Incidentally, to relieve any concern about the possible harm the creature may have suffered from the gaff pole, I should add that the fisherman assured me that the "poke" didn't hurt the beast in the slightest.

A second sighting by the Monterey fisherman who told the preceding tale took place between Twin Rocks (north of the Big Sur coast's famed Bixby Creek Bridge) and the Monterey Peninsula. The sighting occurred in the fall of the year sometime in the late 1930s or early 40s. The time was between 8:00 and 9:00 a.m., and the weather was described as clear and calm.

Because the beast was seen from a distance of approximately 200 yards, there are no details of its facial features or body size. About all that can be said with any degree of accuracy is that the creature was big, alive, and "looked like an upright barrel on the surface." The head appeared to rise from the water a distance of three to four feet. Four or five crew members saw the beast, and the vessel from which it was observed was of the purse seiner variety.

Although the information in this account is sketchy, it is worth documenting because of the description that likened the creature to a barrel. As will be apparent later in this work, the "barrel-like" description offered by this long-time fisherman is not the only such sighting made along the Monterey County coast.

Also of interest to this story is the fisherman's report that one of the crew members grabbed a rifle from the boat's cabin and fired at the distant beast. Seeing a splash in front of the creature, the teller of this tale suspects the shot missed, unless the creature was hit by a ricocheting or "skipping" bullet.

The fisherman went on to say that, given the distance and the small caliber of the gun, the barrel-headed beast probably escaped unhurt even if by chance it *was* hit by the ricocheting bullet. In any event, after the shot the creature wisely dropped from sight, leaving behind another mystery to baffle the men who traverse the waters of California's central coast.

Chapter 5

MONSTER SIGHTINGS IN CARMEL BAY

On the south shore of the Monterey Peninsula lies a second rounded bay. Situated between world-famed Pebble Beach and the beautiful Point Lobos Reserve, the shoreline of this sheltered bay is praised by visitors for its white sandy beaches, its quaint waterfront homes, and its wind-sculptured cypress trees. Known to millions as Carmel Bay, this central California inlet has a charm and beauty that have made it a favorite vacation spot for people from throughout the world.

Despite its popularity, Carmel Bay also boasts a feature that is relatively unknown. Like its larger neighbor to the north, the bay has its own underwater canyon. Leading away from one of the bay's many beaches, the Carmel Trench ultimately joins the larger Monterey Submarine Canyon.

Perhaps even less well-known is a sea monster of sorts that is said to have followed this Carmel Bay canyon to its picturesque shore, where it lolled in the surf before turning tail and heading toward the open sea. Observed by several spectators, this 1948 phenomenon was described quite colorfully in a Monterey newspaper, as well as in a popular Monterey Peninsula magazine. As stated in the magazine, the monster ventured very close to shore (to the first line of breakers, approximately 40 feet from the beach), where it was minutely studied through binoculars. The article provided this detailed description of the beast:

> It was shaped like a huge crook-necked squash some forty feet long and about twelve feet wide through the belly section. It was covered with a mottled pelt of grayish green hair studded with barnacles. It had a long, pinkish, wrinkled neck and head. A row of sharp, glassy bottle-green spines stuck up along its back almost two feet high. It seemed to swim by humping itself along like a serpent. It blew spume out of its mouth or head when it surfaced.

Additional descriptions depicted the creature's tail as vertical—something of a cross between the tail of a whale and that of a shark—while the pinkish head was compared to that of a giant snake or turtle.

The day the sighting was made was stormy, and the seas were reported to be running high. Even though the day was dark and gloomy, numerous well-known and respected Monterey Peninsula residents observed the huge beast as it lolled in the surf. As is usually the case when monsters are spotted, not one of the spectators had a camera. Fortunately, however, a local artist was among the awed spectators and—after considerable coaxing by his friends—took it upon himself to paint a picture of the creature as he remembered it.

Acknowledged as an accurate likeness by a number of witnesses, the picture, along with descriptions of the beast, was presented to marine biologists and their co-workers at Hopkins Marine Station in nearby Pacific Grove. The findings of the experts were varied and inconclusive, with an assortment of rather vague identifications being given. In the end, they indicated that the creature could have been anything from a bullet-headed whale (which is said to be extinct) to a rare whale shark (*Rhincodon typus*). The whale shark (actually a shark and not a whale) has been described as the largest fish in the world. These colossal beasts are usually found in tropical waters and are reported to reach over 60 feet in length!

Another expert with some thoughts on the matter was the late marine biologist Edward F. "Doc" Ricketts, well known to John Steinbeck fans for the part he played in the book *Cannery Row*. Ricketts wondered aloud whether the queer Carmel creature could have been an unknown species of pinniped. (Pinnipeds are carnivorous aquatic mammals of various types, including seals and walruses, that have fin-like feet or flippers.)

Unfortunately, the mysterious green-spined, crook-necked beast has never returned to Carmel Bay for further study or positive identification. Perhaps this "forty-foot squash" disappeared arm in arm (or should I say flipper in flipper?) with its Monterey monster cousins to the north and happily lives in the darkened depths of a subaqueous world, reminiscing, at times, about its joyful outing one April day along the scenic shoreline of Carmel Bay.

Accounts of Carmel Bay monsters include a second sighting of a mysterious sea creature that also took place near the Carmel Trench during the latter 1940s (thought to have been 1947). This second bay beast was observed from the Stewart's Cove area of Carmel Point at approximately 7:00 a.m. on a clear and calm fall day.

Spotted by a milkman who was making his early morning deliveries, the creature was described as "bobbing in the bay" near the Carmel River outfall. Stopping his vehicle to get a better look, the astonished Carmelite noted that the beast's head resembled a barrel in both shape and size.

Curious as to what the barrel-headed behemoth was up to, the milkman continued to study the creature. Suddenly, to his surprise, the beast turned its attention toward the Stewart's Cove area and headed in his direction!

As the creature propelled itself in "humping motions" toward the shore, the milkman marveled at its speed and the fact that it kept its head submerged as it swam. Estimating the "snake-like" body—at least what he could see of it—to be in the neighborhood of 15 feet, the milkman watched in fascination as the creature's "dirty yellow" body coils rose to a height of two to three feet as it made its way through the water.

Awed by this once-in-a-lifetime sight, the milkman continued to stare at the beast, counting four to five coils as it humped along. Finally, realizing that the creature's amazing speed was quickly bringing it ever closer to his rocky perch, the concerned Carmelite prepared to make a quick exit—only to see the snake-like serpent drop from sight, never to be seen again.

Having been an outdoorsman all his life, as well as a talented hunter and fisherman, the milkman was quite adamant about what he saw, and I had no reason to doubt his story when he shared this account with me.

On the opposite shore from the place where the Carmel Trench has its beginning, a third Carmel Bay monster of the 1940s was spotted. A unique aspect of this story, and one that makes it of more than passing interest to sea monster enthusiasts, is that it offers one possible answer to the long-standing question, "What ever became of the Old Man of Monterey Bay?"

The tale begins in the mid-to-late 1940s, when a Monterey fisherman ventured to Alaska in search of work. Upon spending a fishing season in the Alaskan waters, the Monterey man met a fellow fisherman who hailed from the harbor of San Francisco.

Once the San Franciscan learned that his new friend was from the Monterey Peninsula, the subject of their talk soon centered around a strange experience he had had while shark fishing in the Monterey area. As the story was relayed to the Montereyan (who shared it with me in 1979), the San Franciscan and his fellow fishermen favored spending the night in Stillwater Cove over any other inlet in the area. (For those unfamiliar with the Monterey Peninsula, Stillwater Cove borders Pebble Beach, on the north shore of Carmel Bay.)

The adventure began one dark and still night when the shark fishermen were anchored in the picturesque cove. Suddenly the stillness of a boat at rest was broken by strange sounds near the side of the vessel. Upon glancing in the direction from which the sounds came, all aboard the boat were shocked to see a man-like creature of huge proportions rise from the water!

The fishermen gaped in awe at the human-like sea beast, which merely stared back at the frightened men. Finally, after "scaring the daylights" out of the shark boat crew, the mysterious monster dropped from sight as suddenly as it had appeared.

After a sleepless night the fishermen put in another tiring day at sea and then—with apprehension, but driven by curiosity—returned to Stillwater Cove for a second night's stay. Exhausted from their day of fishing, the subdued crew talked in hushed tones and wondered whether they would experience a second visitation from the

nightmarish creature they had encountered the night before. As it turned out they did not have long to wait, as a monstrous human-like head soon rose from the sea!

This second encounter proved too much for one of the crew. Instead of staring in awed silence as the men had done before, the frightened fisherman panicked at the sight of the grotesque creature. Grabbing a gun, he shot the beast as it emerged from the water!

Sinking into the ink-black sea, the creature disappeared from sight. In concluding, the teller of this tale stated that the San Francisco fishermen—turned monster killers—never again saw the nautical nightmare of Stillwater Cove.

With this episode ending on a somewhat somber note, I should add that even though the location, the shooting, and the description of the sea beast are all based on what I believe is an actual incident, I have considerable doubt whether the shooting actually killed the creature. Although the man-like monster was reportedly close to shore when it was supposedly shot, in checking old records and interviewing reliable residents (many of whom had lived in the area for a lengthy period of time), I could find no reports of any mysterious sea beasts—especially one boasting human-like qualities—washing up on the shore of Stillwater Cove or Carmel Bay. With these thoughts in mind, fans of the similar-sounding Old Man of Monterey Bay can rest more easily, knowing that—whatever its fate—it most likely did not meet its end at the hands of a terror-stricken fisherman in Stillwater Cove.

Chapter 6

RED-HEADED SEA SERPENTS AND OTHER TALES

I could go on with additional sea monster sightings that have taken place in and around the bays of Monterey and Carmel, but in most cases they would add little more than numbers to the reports already recounted in these pages. Apart from such mysterious apparitions, Monterey Bay is also known in some circles for the objects that have *disappeared* from its surface. (Readers may recall the young fisherman mentioned in Chapter 3 whose fright upon spotting an apparent sea monster was aroused in part by stories of men and boats that had unaccountably vanished from the waters of the bay.)

One noted marine biologist lends some support to tales of mysterious disappearances. According to this respected scientist, "Anything left on top [of the Trench] for any period of time disappears." In elaborating on this statement, he hinted that items that vanish beneath the surface must somehow be dragged to the bottom, as they are never found washed up on the beaches or nearby shores. Although this scientist did not include boats and men in the list of objects that have been known to be lost—perhaps because they do not remain stationary for long enough periods of time—he did mention such sizable things as missing markers and buoys that have been swallowed up by the bay.

This report by a well-known local scientist adds a certain credibility to the story told to me by a long-time Monterey mariner, who has his own explanation for what may have become of objects that have disappeared without a trace. According to this individual, when the conditions are right a whirlpool forms between the harbors of Monterey and Moss Landing. The old-timer suggested that the small boats that have occasionally been reported missing in Monterey Bay had become caught in this swirl of wild water. Although the existence of a whirlpool of this magnitude is doubtful at best, tales of vanishing objects only add to the mystique of Monterey's picturesque bay.

To add to the list of strange happenings associated with the bay—and as proof that peculiar things have not taken place only in "recent times" (as some people seem to think)—a report from a Santa Cruz newspaper of the 1870s is of interest here. The newspaper account tells of a "new and unknown variety of fish" being caught at Moss Landing. As if "large numbers" of unidentifiable fish being caught near the mouth of Monterey Bay's submarine canyon isn't newsworthy on its own, the fact that the event was at least partially blamed on the "near approach" of a "new comet" makes the incident of even more interest.

Backing up still further, and this time quoting from a San Francisco newspaper of the 1850s, it seems that the bay of Monterey produced a "monster of the lower deep." While not large—measuring only a little over five feet in length—the weird beast appeared to be "a compound of snake, eel and mermaid." To top the description off, the article went on to say that the creature's "countenance" was "strikingly human"!

Perhaps of more importance, as far as sea monsters of the 1850s are concerned, was a Pacific Ocean catch by the whaling ship *Monongahela*, out of the New England whaling port of New Bedford. Even though the capture of the beast took place far from Monterey Bay, it helps to remind us that sea monster sagas have long been part of the nautical lore of the Pacific, as well as that of the Atlantic. The creature was said to be over 100 feet in length and approximately half that in width at its widest point. It was harpooned in mid-ocean, and, after a long chase, it was caught—dead! According to the sailors who inspected the mammoth monster, it boasted two blow holes, four swim fins, an alligator-like head (perhaps similar to Monterey Bay's crocodile-like creature), and 94 very sharp teeth!

After a thorough examination, the whalers cut off the creature's head and preserved it in a pickle barrel. They also rendered the body blubber for oil. News of their adventure was passed to the captain of a homeward-bound ship, and the whalers and their craft went on their way—only to meet a mysterious and presumably deadly fate. Perhaps, as the sailors at home whispered when they heard the story, the sea monster was a "Jonah" that had brought bad luck to the ship. Whatever the cause, the *Monongahela* was never heard from again! Nor was any trace of it ever found—except for the nameboard of the ill-fated vessel, which was found, years later, on the shore of an Aleutian Island.

In returning to stories about Monterey Bay, one sighting of a local Bobo-like beast is of special interest to me, both because the sighting was made by a greatly respected Monterey fisherman and because his account serves as an introduction to the story of a rare serpent-like fish that was caught in the waters of Monterey Bay.

In the fall of 1934, my fisherman acquaintance was at the wheel of the purse seiner *St. Joseph* when he saw what appeared to be a log sticking out of the water. Fully aware of the damage such an object could do, the fisherman cautiously maneuvered around it. When he was about 50 feet away, the object turned in the water and faced the vessel. Startled by the sudden movement of what he thought was a log, the fisherman took a closer look. His surprise turned to shock as he realized that—whatever it was—the log was human-like in appearance and alive!

Not knowing what to do, the fisherman checked the boat's heading to make sure it wouldn't ram the beast and then raced for the galley to tell the crew. Unfortunately, by the time the crew burst onto the deck to see the man-like monster, the creature had disappeared.

In reminiscing about that memorable day, the fisherman stated that the sighting took place in a northwesterly direction from Moss Landing, near (but not over) the Monterey Trench. The depth of the water was about 18 fathoms (approximately 108 feet). The sighting was made in the late evening, and the weather was clear and calm. Bobo, as the fisherman referred to the beast, stuck his head out of the water between two and three feet, and other than being man-like in appearance it was dark in color.

As readers will recognize, this account—while interesting—is not unlike a number of other "Bobo" sightings. What sets this story apart is the fisherman's startling answer when I asked him whether the creature had hair. After thinking for a moment, he replied in the affirmative, saying that "it had reddish colored hair" that "hung straight down."

What excited me about this statement was that over the years I had heard several reports of local "red-headed sea beasts," but I had never been able to talk to anyone who had actually seen one. With the sighting of such a creature now confirmed by a most knowledgeable and respected man, I came to believe that past sightings of red-headed (or red-maned) Monterey Bay monsters should be taken more seriously.

In continuing with reports of red-headed sea beasts of Monterey Bay, I should mention that those who were in the habit of scoffing at stories of Bobo—and other local marine-oriented oddities—laughed heartily when the long-ago accounts of red hair were reported. The skeptics wondered aloud what adornment would be added next to the colorful creature. Others, not quite so easily amused, scratched their heads in bewilderment and attempted to attribute the red hair to seaweed the monster may have become entangled in when it surfaced from the depths of the bay. Those who had actually observed the red-headed beast and its fiery red hair refused to listen either to the jesting or to the theories offered by their bewildered waterfront friends. The vivid red color of the hair, they maintained, was unlike any seaweed they had ever seen. And one must admit that a shock of red hair is not the sort of detail people are likely to invent as a feature of a sea monster.

In checking into the stories of Monterey Bay's flaming-haired serpent, I have discovered a surprising number of supportive facts. Perhaps most important is information indicating that red-headed sea monsters have been reported for as long as man can remember. With confirmed sightings of such creatures coming from many parts of the globe, it is not too much to assume that similar beasts might sometimes inhabit—or at least visit—the deep-water bay of Monterey.

As to what the strange creatures are, scientists from various parts of the world generally agree that the flaming-haired "sea serpent" is a snake-like fish of the *Trachypteridae* family, more commonly referred to as an oarfish. (The oarfish is also sometimes called—perhaps not totally accurately from a marine biologist's point of view—a ribbon fish.) Although quite rare, oarfish are said to inhabit both the Atlantic and Pacific oceans. Mentioned in numerous publications, they are described as being gentle and among the strangest of all sea creatures. In the book *Water Monsters,* Michael Chester explains how they can indeed resemble sea serpents with an adornment of red hair:

> A person who reported seeing a creature with all the characteristics of an oarfish might be suspected of having hallucinations. This fish is a very narrow creature—like a ribbon. It measures as much as 40 to 50 feet in length. It is a bluish-silver color, with a flaming red mane. Of course, its mane is not a mane of hair, but is a modified dorsal fin. An oarfish, rippling through the sea, would look like a giant sea serpent.

The book *Monsters of the Sea,* by Barbara Lindsay, also discusses the "ribbonlike oarfish." In it she tells about one well-known legend that describes a "sixty-foot sea serpent with a snake-like head and mane on its back." The author goes on to say that an oarfish could easily have been mistaken for such a sea serpent, as it too has a mane, "a red crest on the top of its head that stiffens and stands up when the oarfish is alarmed."

Again, in the book *A History of Fishes,* J. R. Norman shares some interesting information about the peculiar oarfish:

The monster described as having the head of a horse with flaming red mane is the oarfish or ribbon fish, a species which probably grows to more than 50 feet in length, and may sometimes be seen swimming with undulating movements at the surface of the sea. The famous Sea Serpent, measuring 56 feet in length, that was cast upon the shore of Orkney [Scotland] in 1808 was almost certainly this fish.

There is ample verification, then, that lengthy serpent-like creatures with a reddish crest or mane do in fact inhabit our oceans. Inasmuch as these beasts swim with a snake-like, undulating motion—carrying part of their head above the water, as stated in *The World Book Encyclopedia*—one can't help but wonder whether Monterey Bay's red-headed "Old Man" might have been a giant fish of the oarfish variety.

Additional evidence bearing on this interesting possibility can be found in the files of the Santa Cruz City Museum. As stated in the museum commission minutes of June 5, 1942:

In the early part of '38, a rare, deep water fish was caught in our local bay, and turned over as an oddity, to Mr. Turver [the museum director], who had it put on ice. It became a matter of study and speculation to a group of nature lovers, and through them the Smithsonian Institute at Washington got wind of it. The Institute was deeply interested, and wanted it for its collection. Only twice before had it known of such a catch, and these were comparatively small and mutilated.

It had been Mr. Turver's intention to make a cast of the fish for our Museum, as the best method of exhibiting it locally. He now replied to the Smithsonian that it could have the fish in exchange for a cast. "Agreed," said the Smithsonian. Mr. Turver and Mr. Strohbeen packed it in 105 lbs. of dry ice. Mr. Pendleton carted it over the mountains to catch the east bound train at San Jose. And in early March 1941, it became the coveted possession of Uncle Sam at the Smithsonian.

Some months later, true to promise, the very carefully-made and beautiful cast, in natural colors even to the sheen of the skin, arrived in Santa Cruz. Since then, out of odd bits of time and as a labor of love, Mr. Turver, in his home shop, made for it a fitting case. Last night Mr. Turver and Mr. Strohbeen put it in position. Today the people of Santa Cruz share with the Smithsonian the distinction of being the only possessors in America, possibly in the world, of a Museum exhibit of a six-foot ribbon fish, drawn from the depths of the sea—in this case, from 600 feet below surface level.

While not a monster 50 feet long, the Santa Cruz specimen serves as proof that the extremely rare ribbon fish has visited (or even inhabited) the waters of Monterey Bay. On display to this day in the Santa Cruz City Museum, the beautifully prepared cast adds considerable credibility to the long-scoffed-at stories of red-headed sea beasts in our local waters. With numerous reports indicating that fish of the oarfish variety are capable of growing to a length approximately 10 times that of the Santa Cruz specimen, the possibility cannot be discounted that at one time there may have been fish in Monterey Bay that boasted flaming red manes, were snake-like in appearance, and grew to monstrous proportions!

Chapter 7

THE MONSTER
OF MOORE'S BEACH

As I approach the end of this collection of tales about the elusive monsters of the Monterey Bay area, it's time to tell about one "monster" that *didn't* get away. Often, when the subject of sea monsters comes up, the end of the tale tells how the creature majestically swam out to sea, or mysteriously submerged in a pool of inky black. However, in rare cases there have been reports of remarkable beasts of the deep that have washed onto the world's distant beaches. Two cases in point that have previously been described are Verrill's 200-foot *Octopus giganteus* and the 56-foot sea serpent (or oarfish/ribbon fish) that was cast upon the Orkney shores over a century and a half ago.

Not to be outdone, Monterey Bay, too, boasts a beast of monstrous proportions whose carcass was found on its rocky north shore. The year was 1925, the place was Moore's Beach (now a part of the Natural Bridges State Beach), and the discoverer was Charles Moore.

Dramatically described in numerous newspapers, the creature became the talk of California's central coast. With the story continuing to make front-page news, people from far and near made their way to Moore's Beach to see the "Santa Cruz serpent." Before long descriptions of the monster were almost as plentiful as the number of people

63

who came to view it. To give an idea of how these descriptions varied, and how the monster looked to different individuals, a few of the descriptions are included here.

The first account is from a well-known Monterey merchant of more than 60 years ago. In telling about the "serpent-like monster," he said it was approximately 50 feet long and 2 feet in diameter. Its head resembled a duck, while its tail looked like a fish. Perhaps the strangest feature of all, as indicated by this Monterey man, were "elephant-like legs every few yards along the body," complete with a plentiful supply of "ivory toenails"!

A second description, from the *Monterey Peninsula Herald,* refers to the Santa Cruz serpent as a "freak of Father Neptune." The article goes on to say that it reached a length of 35 feet and a height of 5 feet. It possessed a duck-shaped head and a tail like a whale. Interestingly, and perhaps closer to the truth than many of the other accounts, the description also said that the monster possessed "an odor which kept curious ones at a respectful distance." Finally, the newspaper stated that geologists, paleontologists, anthropologists, and deep-sea divers were to be asked to give the creature "a close inspection."

According to another story, this one in the *Santa Cruz News,* the mystery monster was 34 feet long, its head was bigger than a barrel, its mouth resembled a duck's bill, and its eyes were bigger than abalones. In continuing, the newspaper stated the beast had a great oval-shaped body with a neck 7 feet long and 36 inches in diameter. Among the strangest of the creature's features, as reported in this account, was the fact that the beast's body was covered with a coat of "semi-hair and feathers"!

Bernard Heuvelmans, in his previously mentioned book *In the Wake of the Sea Serpents,* discusses the monster in the following terms: "It was a strange creature, with a huge head longer than a man, tiny eyes and sort of duck's head

The Moore's Beach monster is truly one that didn't get away. Below the fold of the neck, an elephant-like leg—complete with ivory toenails—can be seen. Legs of this type were reported by a Monterey merchant to have been "every few yards along the body." This photograph is included at this point as proof to doubters that strange and rare creatures of the deep *do* frequent the waters of California's central coast. Photo credit – Dorothy C. Miller beak. It was joined to the main body by a slender neck that seemed to be about thirty feet long."

So much for descriptions of the strange beast. As for identifying the monster, numerous people—some of them knowledgeable—and others less so—were only too ready to offer their theories. Among them was E. L. Wallace of Santa Cruz, who was twice president of the Natural History Society of British Columbia. In reference to the creature Wallace had this to say:

> My examination of the monster was quite thorough. I felt in its mouth and found it had no teeth. Its head is large and its neck fully twenty feet long. The body is weak and the tail is only three feet in length from the end of the backbone. These facts do away with the whale theory [which had been proposed by a handful of authorities], as the backbone of a whale is far larger than any bone in this animal. Again its tail is too weak for an animal of the deep and does away with that last version.
>
> With a bill like it possesses, it must have lived on herbage and undoubtedly inhabited a swamp. I would call it a type of plesiosaurus [a sea reptile of prehistoric times].

After further examination, Wallace also theorized that the antique monster might have been preserved in a glacier for countless years. After being released by the gradual melting of the ice, he speculated, the beast might have floated into warmer water, where it was eventually cast upon the Santa Cruz shore.

Another interesting observation that fits into the prehistoric monster category was offered by the respected Santa Cruz judge W. R. Springer. Judge Springer was unsure as which classification of prehistoric animal the monster belonged to, but he felt certain that it was a monster from a past age, "perhaps millions of years old." In describing the creature he spoke of its duck-like head and 20-foot-long neck. He also mentioned evidence of two short feet (or flippers, or fins) beneath the beast's "ugly gigantic head."

In continuing, Judge Springer discussed how the reptile must have swum with its head high above the water, presenting a formidable sight to any sailor who had the misfortune of viewing it from the watch house. In a Santa Cruz newspaper of 1925, the respected judge stated:

> A monstrosity of the sea would probably best describe the strange creature. Should such a head as it possesses be protruded over the rail of a vessel it should be enough to put the hardest kind of an old tar on the water wagon for life.

With so-called positive identifications continuing to pour in, the mysterious monster of Moore's Beach was confidently referred to as—among other things—a bottle-neck whale, a bottle-nosed whale, a box-nosed walrus, a shovel-bill shark, and a bottle-nosed porpoise.

While the "experts" continued to brand the beast with assorted titles, the *Santa Cruz Sentinel* added interest to the sea serpent saga with an account of a "terrific battle" that had taken place a few days before the discovery of the Moore's Beach monster—a battle between a dozen or more sea lions and a gigantic fish! According to the article, a Mr. E. J. Lear had observed the incident near Santa Cruz's Houghton Beach. As stated by Lear:

> I was driving a team toward Capitola [a neighboring Santa Cruz community] and suddenly I was attracted by some young sea lions not far out. They were lined up and several large lions were swimming back and forth in front of them. Much farther out I saw the water being churned to foam and thrown high up in the air, and then all of a sudden a

big form shot into the air. It was shiny and I took it for a big fish. A dozen or more sea lions were battling it, and every once in a while all would raise out of the water. It looked to me as though all the sea lions were attacking it beneath as the monster came out of the water several times. In telling [of] the battle of that night I estimated its length at 30 feet.

The battle continued as long as I could see it from the road. I was driving toward Capitola with a load of sand. I have not seen the monster on the beach, but possibly it may have been that which I saw.

Lear's remarkable story added a new layer of mystery to the saga of Moore's Beach. For the residents of Santa Cruz and the entire central coast, this was one sea monster melodrama that was getting better by the day!

With the appearance of the dramatic story of a titanic struggle at sea, and with "positive" identifications continuing to be reported by self-proclaimed authorities, it is little wonder that local interest in the monster of Moore's Beach continued to run at fever pitch. Finally, after several noted scientists scratched their heads (and held their noses) over the duck-billed beast, officials from the California Academy of Sciences (who claimed the body of the creature for scientific study) carefully inspected the mammal's skull and announced their findings to the world. The mysterious monster of Moore's Beach, they asserted, was a North Pacific type of beaked whale. This creature was said to be so rare that no name—except its Latin one, *Berardius bairdi* (given to it by Leonhard Stejneger in 1883)—had ever been bestowed upon it.

With the mystery monster officially given a name, and with further reports suggesting that the dual effects of decomposition and high seas had separated the body from the skin (which, in turn, had rolled up on itself to create the illusion of a long neck), the puzzle of Moore's Beach seemingly was solved. Most area residents nodded in agreement and readily accepted the findings of the California Academy scientists. Still, there were those who refused to believe that the beast was a member of the whale family and steadfastly clung to the theory that the monster was of unknown origin, possibly a throwback to prehistoric times.

These diehards may not have been merely stubborn disbelievers. Of interest here is the information that these events of 1925 predate the discovery of a *true* prehistoric "beast" by 13 years. The creature in question was a coelacanth, an ancient species of fish that many scientists believed had died out more than 50 million years ago. Yet in 1938 just such an "extinct" fish was caught off the coast of South Africa, proving beyond doubt that creatures of prehistoric times *do* exist in our underwater world.

The coelacanth isn't the only "extinct" species of marine life that has been found among the living. A second example is something called a "deep-sea worm-snail," known to scientists as *Neopilina galatheae*. This particular type of worm-snail was thought to have died out more than 300 million years ago. Much to the surprise of people who study such things, in 1952 some were found—alive and well—off the coast of Costa Rica!

Those who debated the origin of the Moore's Beach monster nearly three quarters of a century ago could not have known that future discoveries would lend new support to the idea that prehistoric creatures continue to lurk in the oceans of the world. In a similar way, we who marvel at these "finds" today might be wise to pause and ponder all that is not yet known about the world under the sea and the surprises that new discoveries may bring. With the secrets of Monterey Bay's submarine canyon just beginning to be unlocked, and with heretofore unknown species being brought to light, perhaps a dose of humility before nature's wonders is in order. Perhaps, too, we should be less quick to dismiss reports of strange and unidentifiable creatures in local waters as figments of the imaginations of glory-seeking fishermen.

Having presented the fishermen's tales, and the relevant facts, as accurately as I can, I must leave the verdict up to you. So, readers, what do you think? Have there ever been—and are there now—sea monsters frolicking in the waters of Monterey Bay?

Conclusion

Even though this book is of modest proportions, to the best of my knowledge it is the most complete collection of Monterey Bay area "sea monster" stories that has ever been published. Sadly, many more such tales have been lost forever as many of the fishermen who witnessed odd creatures, and experienced strange happenings, died before anyone thought to record their accounts. Happily, I was able to talk to a number of fishermen before they, too, passed from the scene. The incidents documented in this work are only a sampling of the stories I have collected. Many of the tales I chose to omit are similar in many respects to those I have included. With this in mind, I would like to add that even though I omitted a number of Monterey Bay sightings, I think the incidents described in these pages are a worthy representation of the kinds of reports that have helped to make Monterey Bay and its immediate environs so unique—at least from a sea monster enthusiast's point of view!

With more and more people visiting California's central coast, and with the Monterey Bay National Marine Sanctuary adding a new distinction to this beautiful area, I would like to think that readers of this work will be instrumental in informing those who decide to do a little fishing while they are in the area that they had best check their lines twice. After all, who knows what rare beast may become the "catch of the day"—or the century!

Books by Randall A. Reinstedt

Randall A. Reinstedt's
Paperback Series:

Ghost Notes
Ghostly Tales and Mysterious Happenings of Old Monterey
Ghosts, Bandits and Legends of Old Monterey
Incredible Ghosts of Old Monterey's Hotel Del Monte
Incredible Ghosts of the Big Sur Coast
Monterey's Mother Lode
Mysterious Sea Monsters of California's Central Coast
Shipwrecks and Sea Monsters of California's Central Coast
Tales, Treasures and Pirates of Old Monterey
Where Have All the Sardines Gone?

Randall A. Reinstedt's

History & Happenings of California Series . . .
putting the *story* back in hi*story* for young readers:

Lean John, California's Horseback Hero
One-Eyed Charley, the California Whip
Otters, Octopuses, and Odd Creatures of the Deep
Stagecoach Santa
The Strange Case of the Ghosts of the
  Robert Louis Stevenson House
Tales and Treasures of California's Missions
Tales and Treasures of California's Ranchos
Tales and Treasures of the California Gold Rush

For information on purchasing books contact:

Ghost Town Publications
P.O. Drawer 5998
Carmel, CA 93921
(408) 373-2885